HEART
OF THE
WARRIOR

Paul,

*May you always know
that God is with you
and will
protect you and your family
as you
develop the
Heart of the Warrior.*

Thank you for your willingness to be
a Heart 2 Heart group leader.

Love from your
Walled Lake Family

April 1997

HEART
OF THE
WARRIOR

A BATTLE PLAN FOR CHRISTIAN MEN

Michael O'Donnell

COLLEGE PRESS
PUBLISHING COMPANY
Joplin, Missouri

This book and poem are dedicated to
Joel Lemon
Brother,
Husband,
Father,
& Friend

When God wants to drill a man
And thrill a man
And skill a man,

When God wants to mold a man
To play the noblest part;

When He yearns with all His heart
To create so great and bold a man
That all the world shall be amazed,
Watch His methods, watch His ways!

How He ruthlessly perfects
Whom He royally elects!

How He hammers him and hurts him,
And with mighty blows converts him
Into trial shapes of clay
Which only God understands.

While his tortured heart is crying
And he lifts beseeching hands!

How he bends but never breaks
When His good he undertakes;

How He uses whom He chooses
And with every purpose fuses him;

By every act induces him
To try His splendor out —
God knows what He's about!

Contents

Contents

Introduction

You are about to embark on a wonderful journey toward greater masculinity. No matter what your age — whether you are a father or soon to be one — you will find yourself in the company of brothers who, just like you, desire to take up the Mantle of Manhood. Your common quest will be to hear and receive our King's call to arms. Together with fellow heirs to the Kingdom of God, you will discover what it means to have the heart of a warrior.

You are not here by accident. God called you out of the world to assemble with men, both young and old, to prepare for spiritual warfare. The training will not be easy, but the rewards will be great. You will move from mere infancy to affirmation as a son to eventually a man with purpose. You will get to know yourself, your Lord, and your enemy. And, most importantly, you will have a renewed heart for God and your family that will literally consume you. God's ways will become your ways!

This small group study guide is based on the popular book, *Heart of the Warrior*, now being used by Promise Keepers' Point Men around the country. From its pages, you will learn the importance of seeking out your own "warrior band" — Christian brothers who will stand beside you and wield the weapons of God's arsenal: prayer, confession, and the Word. Study questions related to each chapter will help you understand the value of forming strong bonds with godly men who will help you strengthen your own spiritual resolve and make you a better brother, husband, and dad. You will learn how to become less religious and more spiritual, building your confidence as a capable warrior and forging an ever-strengthening bond with God, your eternal Father. Finally, you'll discover the true definition of masculinity — as personified by Jesus Christ, the ultimate man.

One of the most pivotal persons in the Bible, John the Baptist, had a prophetic mission, stated this way in Luke 1:17: "And he will go on before the Lord, in the spirit and power of Elijah, *to turn the hearts of the fathers to their children*, and the disobedient to the wisdom of the righteous — to make ready a people prepared for the Lord" [italics added].

Men, we must come together with other Christian brothers to put on the spiritual armor God has provided and take on our God-given responsibilities as spiritual leaders in our homes. Like King David and his mighty men, we must gather as modern-day spiritual soldiers to mount a counterattack on mankind's greatest foe: Satan.

Group leaders are free to adapt the review section at the close of each study to their group's needs. Although some questions are specifically devised for group discussion, many could be answered at home between sessions.

Study One
The Heroes Gather

As a way of introduction, read the following Scriptures to better understand the historical background of David and his mighty men:

1. Samuel anoints David to one day be king (1 Sam. 16:12-13)

2. David, now in training, becomes King Saul's armor-bearer (1 Sam. 16:21)

3. King Saul is unfaithful (1 Chron. 10:13)

4. David inquires of the Lord (2 Sam. 2:1)

5. David reigns at Mt. Hebron with Warriors, 7 years and 6 months (2 Sam. 5:4-5)

Read the following from *Heart of the Warrior*:

David rubs dust and sweat from his eyes as he watches two of his warriors test their strength, steel against steel, amidst the shouts and laughter of their rowdy friends.

Uriah slaps David on the back nearly hard enough to knock him from his post among the rocks, then quickly grabs his arm and hauls him back to his perch on the craggy flank of Mount Hermon.

"Some warrior you are, Uriah," David yells above the clamor. "Try it again when I'm looking."

"Another time, my friend," Uriah says, joining David high above the gathered men.

Gazing again across his camp, David recalls with sadness how his warrior friends had recently become bitter and even talked of stoning him when the Amalekites had raided and burned their camp at Ziklag — taking captive their women and children while the men were gone off to war.

David's men became violent and rebellious, turning against one another.

But God gave them the victory over the Amalekites, and they retrieved every person and possession that had been taken from them. In this way, God helped restore the men's loyalty to David and their trust in one another.

These are the men God called? David wonders once again. *What an amazing group God has gathered to serve his purposes!*

There stands Jashobeam, the chief of David's top three fighters, who has wielded his spear against three hundred men — killing them all in one battle. And there are the mighty bowmen who can shoot arrows and sling stones equally well with both hands. Leaning against a stone is the valiant fighter Benaiah, who struck down two of Moab's best men, killed a lion in a snowy pit, and destroyed a seven-and-a-half-foot Egyptian with the giant's own spear.

As David looks upon the strong men who had come to him in exile — many of them even related to David's recent nemesis, King Saul — he smiles. Uriah notices and has to smile himself.

I would die for this man, my King, Uriah thinks. *Here we are, forced away from friends and family, a small band compared to King Saul's vast armies. Yet, God's might is here. God is among us.*

To David's amazement, men continue to pour into his

camp by the hundreds and thousands, preparing the way for him to become king of Israel. Still, he draws his true strength from God and from the small band of warriors who have gathered round him in his early days of exile.

Hidden away in the mountains, the mighty men in that first, small group of fugitives had been forced to depend on each other. As they prepared to do God's work in the land, the Lord changed the brawny, violent men. Now they hunted to help feed others. They fought as a team. They were willing to die for each other. The warriors' might remained, but their loyalty was directed toward David and his God. Each day, as the men grew in strength, they also grew in faith. How could they not love and worship God who continually gave them victory against amazing odds? And how could they not love their commander, whose heart was so close to God's own? (Taken from *Heart of the Warrior*, pp. 1-3.)

After reading this story of David and his mighty men, consider this diagram that contrasts "Men of the World Versus Men of Mount Hebron." (Note all traits on the right side of the diagram are taken from the Hebrew word *Hebron*.)

Men of the World	**Men of Mount Hebron**
Isolation	Intimacy
Lust	Covenant Love
Me	Others
Rejected	Received
Punish	Protect
Aloneness	Alliance
Bitterness	Sweetness
Wasting Away	Built Up
Whipping Oneself	Worshiping God
Rebellion	Unity

It is my belief that God intentionally sent David to Mount Hebron to learn a powerful lesson regarding community and accountability. Manliness includes a pattern for friendship that is characterized by the traits found on the right side of our diagram. Men of the world, like David's mighty men before they were changed on Mt. Hebron, are too often detached, distant, and even dangerous. Without Christian companions to help them, their genuine, Christ-centered nature is lost and their true, God-given call ignored.

Perhaps even you have been experiencing this same bitterness and aloneness. You've been punishing and rejecting yourself. You want to change but in isolation you just don't know how. I believe Mt. Hebron is the key!

We must assemble as men, in a symbolic/spiritual sense, on Mt. Hebron where God's greatest work is yet to be done. Our call is to begin coming together in ever increasing numbers so God can forge a band of spiritual champions whose love and loyalty to each other is surpassed only by our love and loyalty to Jesus Christ.

Such love and loyalty were the ultimate hallmarks of David's mighty men. Let's read further as Uriah studies David as he watches his men hone their battle skills (based on 1 Chron. 11:15-19):

> [Uriah's] heart once again swells with pride and a powerful brotherly love as he recalls the recent feat accomplished by three of his fellow chiefs. David had been in the stronghold when the three came to watch the Philistine garrison at Bethlehem. Their leader longed for water, and wished aloud, "Oh, that someone would get me a drink of water from the well near the gate of Bethlehem."
>
> David was giving no command. He was issuing no

order. He was simply thinking out loud. But David's warriors — his closest friends — rushed from the stronghold, broke through the Philistine lines to Bethlehem, and drew water from the well.

Fighting their way back through fierce Philistine warmongers, the three men arrived once again at David's cave. Breathless and bleeding, they proudly handed David the water. He looked at the cool, clear liquid. He looked at his men, moved beyond words. The future king could not drink the water. Instead, he poured it out before the Lord as a "thank offering."

"God forbid that I should do this!" he said. "Should I drink the blood of these men who went at the risk of their lives?" Such was the incredible love, the extravagant devotion of these heroic men to their leader.

The Lord grafted the heart of David's men to their leader because David had a heart after God's own. In exile, these mighty warriors learned life's most valued lesson: "Greater love has no one than this, that a man lay down his life for his friends" (John 15:13). Their military might did not come from their brawn alone. God's power emanated from their hearts — hearts that were loyal, faithful, and loving — even to the point of death. (Taken from *Heart of the Warrior*, pp. 3-4.)

I have a dear friend, Paul Schumann, who recently shared with me that women come together to communicate whereas men come together to fight battles. I think he's hit upon an important gender distinction — one that may well help to explain why men have not banded together in our generation quite like women have. You see, we don't know that there's a battle to be fought and a victory to be won! We've simply not heard God's call to arms.

In wartime trivial differences vanish. Men make war buddies for life. Young husbands and wives suddenly feel a renewed commitment to one another when they are afraid they could be separated forever through death at the hands of a common enemy.

A young father recently watched a television documentary about the 8th Air Force, stationed in England during World War II. His father was a part of that close-knit group of airmen.

"It almost made me wish I had a chance to go to war — to share in that camaraderie, that special closeness men shared," he said. "World War II defined the men of my father's generation. They had a mission, a common enemy. Watching them fly sorties into Nazi-occupied territories and into Hitler's Germany . . . it was magnificent and terrible all at the same time. The Air Force took tremendous losses. But all those brave, young men were part of one team. They were brothers. They were willing to die for each other without a thought. Watching there in my living room, I was so moved. I almost wished I could join them."

Men, we can have this same closeness without the bloodshed! Satan is waging a war so dreadful that Christian men must draw upon one another's strength to fight him. Satan is real, the battle is real, and the outcome will determine the fate of our souls and the souls of our wives and children. (Taken from *Heart of the Warrior*, p. 7.)

Reflecting on Study One

1. As an icebreaker, take an item out of your wallet that says something about you and share it with the whole group.

2. As you consider the prescribed historical review at the beginning of the chapter, compare and contrast David and King Saul.

3. Why do you think God considered faithfulness, inquiry, and obedience of him to be such important qualities for the man who would be king?

4. When looking at the diagram, "Men of the World Versus Men of Mount Hebron," which side would you place yourself on and why?

5. Discuss how the idea of "lust" differs from the concept of "covenant love."

6. Discuss how the "rejection of self" versus "the protection of self by others" is a missing dynamic in the church today.

7. Do you find it interesting that when men are not "whipping themselves" they are "worshiping God"? What are some of the possible implications here?

8. The terms "sweetness" and "pleasant" are used

interchangeably in the Hebrew language. Read Psalm 133 and tell the group what you find and why the fact that David wrote this psalm is significant.

9. Read the story of Jonathan and his armor-bearer as found in 1 Samuel 14:1-23 and discuss what valuable lessons can be learned from it.

10. How is Paul's language in 1 Corinthians 13 an important parallel to David's men displaying sacrificial love as the basis for community?

Study Two
The Battleground

Meet Hank. He appears to be in his late 50s — steel-gray hair, face lined by a lifetime of frustration and worry. He carries himself with an air of distinction, but the slight slump of his shoulders and the strained smile tell you he's deeply troubled.

Hank discovered how easily Satan can ambush our families — harming our wives and children. We want to share his story with you, for Hank was one of the walking wounded.

"Jan and I met and married at a Christian college during the early '50s," Hank begins. "We were both from homes where the Bible was believed, where church attendance was required, but where grace and genuine caring were largely absent.

"My father was a depression-era man: he worked hard to put food on the table and buy what we needed, but he spent so much energy meeting our physical needs that he had nothing left over to offer us spiritually. When I look back now, I guess I never learned a whole lot about masculine involvement in the lives of children.

"Not too long after our babies started coming along, I was diagnosed with a serious illness — compounded, the doctor said, by the stress I was under. My physician told me to reduce the amount of pressure in my life, so most day-to-day responsibilities for managing our household fell onto Jan. She became Mom, Dad, house-keeper, budgeter, shopper, disciplinarian, schedule-keeper, car-pooler — well, everything.

"My role was reduced to little more than cheerleader, buddy and sympathetic shoulder-to-cry-on for my children. Before long, I realize now, the kids began resenting Jan. Forced into a role she didn't really want, and without emotional or spiritual backing from me, she was forced to do everything on her own. She was over-burdened, tired and stressed — and all that strain came through in the ways she dealt with the children.

"The kids saw her as domineering, critical, and short-tempered. I was just grateful she was there, but I felt so helpless. As she took on more and more of the responsibilities for our family, we talked less and grew further apart. When the kids began to complain about all her rules and schedules, I let them blow off steam with me. I didn't stand up for her.

"Through the years, they treated Jan with less and less respect. Although they obviously loved us both, I was the favorite. Jan was the disciplinarian; I was the pal. Even as they grew up, married and had children of their own, Jan was often sad because she was not close to the kids like I was."

Fortunately, the story doesn't end here. Hank decided to reclaim his family after all the years of reckless abandon. He knew it would not be easy. He began to pray about it with a close friend, and prayer with his friend led to prayer with Jan. As they prayed together to ask God to bind the enemy in their lives, insight began to come to them in extraordinary ways.

"I had a dream last night," Jan told Hank on one occasion. "It was disturbing. We were with our children and grandchildren for some holiday gathering but I couldn't come out of the bedroom to be with you all."

"Why not?"

"Well, frankly, I didn't have any clothes to wear. And I wasn't about to parade in front of the children naked."

"What an odd dream," said Hank.

"Even stranger is that I've had the dream more than once. And every time it occurs I feel more and more uncomfortable inside. I wonder what it means?"

Hank decided to share the dream with his close friend and prayer partner. Without hesitation, his friend offered a possible explanation:

"Perhaps the dream refers to your upcoming trip to Dallas to visit with your family for Christmas. Jan's lack of clothes to wear could be symbolic of her feelings of vulnerability. Didn't you tell me that earlier in your marriage you abandoned your role as the spiritual head of your home?"

Hank sadly agreed.

"Years of not providing a daily prayer covering for Jan," the friend continued, "coupled with allowing her to assume all spiritual responsibilities, possibly has left her feeling unprotected from Satan's attacks — and vulnerable to critical, cutting remarks from your kids. This holiday, God may be calling you to spend time reclaiming your family and resuming the role of spiritual head and protector of your wife once again."

"It all makes so much sense," Hank confessed, nodding slowly in agreement.

Hank and Jan gathered friends and loved ones about them for prayers concerning their upcoming trip to Dallas. Men of Hank's congregation prayed for God to empower him to engage the enemy in his home. They prayed for Satan's binding in Hank's now-grown children and asked that the children be loosed to God's will and his ways through Hank's leadership.

Satan is powerful. He did not give up his stronghold on this family right away.

"We were looking for just the right opportunity to speak

to the entire family," Hank said. "But as Satan would have it, all the grandchildren were ill. Their sickness required their parents' time and attention — the very time and attention we so desperately craved to talk with them. The weekend was almost over."

Hank called his prayer partner long distance.

"We need to ask God to bind the enemy," he said, feeling a growing sense of desperation. "Satan has attacked the grandchildren with illnesses so that we can't find the time for me to speak."

They prayed and fasted. Satan was defeated. The grandchildren slept or were comforted, and their parents were available once again.

Hank approached his family and asked for their forgiveness for having abandoned his God-given responsibility as the spiritual head of the home. He told them that whatever debt they felt their mother owed them, he now took upon himself. He assumed responsibility for her indebtedness.

Hank told them he would no longer listen to critical or hurtful remarks about how they had been reared. He then prayed over them and blessed them. To the praise of God, they have not been the same since. (Taken from *Heart of the Warrior*, pp. 9-12.)

Maybe you can relate to Hank. His plight is not new. Many men confess that they leave much of what goes on at home to their wives. "It's just part of the culture," they tell us, "in which men are breadwinners — nothing more, nothing less." As far as headship in the home is concerned, men are either passive and irresponsible — like Hank — or domineering and insensitive. There seems to be no middle ground on this battlefield of life.

But in our true story above, hanging out with a prayer partner began to change all that. Hank got wise to the tactics of Satan and decided to do something about it. Turning to a Christian brother for counsel and advice was a major step forward in the right direction. Hank soon realized he couldn't go it alone. And when "two of you agree on earth concerning anything that you ask, it will be done for you by my Father in heaven" (Matt. 18:19).

Men who come together with other men to form a community of spiritual strength are not unlike David and his mighty men who took back the kingdom from Saul, or Jonathan and his armor-bearer who, although ridiculously outnumbered, crushed hundreds of Philistines with the power of God in their midst. As men created in the image of God this should no longer surprise us. Doesn't Proverbs tell us, "As iron sharpens iron, so one man sharpens another" (27:17)?

Let's think about Moses for a minute.

Moses, like men today, was called to do the impossible. He was to be a father, prophet, and priest to the house of Israel. And when God began to reveal his plans for a mighty nation under his leadership, Moses felt that basic insecurity common to man; that terrible feeling of inadequacy; that gnawing in your gut that says, "You can't, so why even try?"

But God comforted Moses with just two words, "I AM."

Modern-day warriors are beginning to understand the all-sufficiency of that ancient phrase: "For where two or three come together in my name, there I AM in the midst of them" (Matt. 18:20).

Between two or three men who intentionally gather to wage war against a formidable foe — Satan — is God, himself, who literally raised Jesus Christ from the grave! His power is available to us today. And this power will help us to lead in our homes, churches, and communities. Failure to do so will impact future generations to come.

In the movie *Aliens 2*, a young lieutenant in an armored personnel carrier stands frozen as his crew screams in agony nearby. They are being attacked by savage, alien beings and need to be rescued immediately. He's paralyzed with shock. He does nothing.

Finally, in desperation, a woman who is not even a member of the military crew shoves him aside and drives the vehicle straight through the walls to rescue the wounded and bleeding before they are killed.

The woman in the movie was not trying to be a hero. She was just trying to do the right thing, the only way she knew how. She was forced into an unwelcomed role because the man who was supposed to be leading *failed to lead*. (Taken from *Heart of the Warrior*, pp. 14-15.)

Unlike at the movies, our battleground is real. Every day, for example, print media run the following headlines:

✧ "Where's Dad? Not at Home" —*USA Today*

✧ "Now Who Gets the Blame . . . ? Dear Old Dad" —*Newsweek*

✧ "Fatherless America" —*USA Weekend*

✧ "Life Without Father" —*New York Times*

✧ "Do We Really Need Fathers?" — *Christianity Today*

The simple fact is in the 1960s, "in the Age of Ozzie and Harriet, 17 percent of children lived apart from their fathers. Today, in the Age of Murphy Brown, that figure has reached nearly 40 percent" (*The Christian Science Monitor*, Thursday, November 3, 1994). Other statistics are equally grim and that spells trouble!

Consider God's warning to future generations if Dad allows his heart to wander. "See, I will send you the prophet . . . he will turn the hearts of the fathers to their children . . . or else I will come and strike the land with a curse" (Mal. 4:6). Now let me ask you, "Has God smitten our land with a curse?" You bet, and it's high time men did something about it. Men like Hank who, even late in life, decide to reach out to at least one other friend and ask, "Brother, can you spare me some time?" Men, like the ones you're meeting with now, who want to say "yes" to their families and "no" to the world. May God bless you!

Men, God has given us clear commands to not only love our wives but to give them a protective prayer covering against evil and hurt and pain. We must not allow our wives to be unprotected from the evil that daily tries to invade our homes, our lives, and the lives of our children. As we grow in our own spirituality — with the strength and encouragement of our prayer brothers and our families — we can become the mighty warriors for the Lord with hearts after his own.

This is your first step to develop the heart of a warrior. Your personal prayers to God are vital. Your closeness and friendship with your wife is as important as ever. But you may have powerful sins or temptations your wife doesn't understand or can't help you overcome. And maybe you've prayed again and again on your own, but when the next day's stresses hit — you backslide. Who better to help you fight these battles than other Christian brothers, men you would trust with your life?

God encourages men to unite in their faith. He is calling you to join with other Christian heroes who are ready to heed his call to arms. (Taken from *Heart of the Warrior,* pp. 16-17.)

Reflecting on Study Two

1. When reading about Hank, can you see any of yourself in him before his change of heart?

2. Think about the story of Boaz and Ruth in the Old Testament. How is the fact that Boaz was a "kinsman-redeemer" similar to Hank assuming his wife's debt in the eyes of his children?

3. How is being a "kinsman-redeemer" similar to Christ's role with the church?

4. Review Malachi 4:5-6 and Luke 1:17 and discuss the significance of these passages of Scripture.

5. Margaret Meade, a child development expert, has said, "Men are a biological necessity, but a social accident." Reflect on her comment and discuss whether you agree or disagree.

6. Other than *Aliens 2*, what films depict the abdication of responsibility or leadership on the part of males?

7. Read Psalm 78:1-8 and relate it to the idea of "intergenerational pathology" (that is, if my father abused my mother I may well abuse my wife, etc.). What can we learn about our duty as men and fathers from this text? How do we break the cycle of sins passed on from one generation to the next?

8. Reflect on the TV image of today's men, husbands, and fathers. How has their depiction changed since you were a boy?

9. What do you think about women becoming "heroes" when men fail to lead?

10. Do you think there is "father hunger" (that is, the idea of searching for a father figure) in America today? How is that hunger expressed in contemporary terms? How about in ancient terms (refer to John 20:10 and following, with particular attention given to verse 17)?

Study Three
The Warriors Unite

The following account of David and Bathsheba is adapted into story form from 2 Samuel 11:

In the spring, at the time when kings go off to war, David sends his commander, Joab, out with the king's mighty men and the whole Israelite army. They destroy the Ammonites and besiege Rabbah. But King David chooses to remain behind in Jerusalem, isolating himself from the warriors who are his closest friends.

One evening the king, restless and bored, gets up from his bed and walks around on the roof of the palace. From his high position he sees a beautiful woman bathing. He looks away, out over the city. But soon his eyes are drawn to her dark loveliness, the water pouring over her bare shoulders. Her hair gleams in the moonlight.

And why shouldn't I look upon this woman as I do my own city! David thinks to himself. *I am the king of all Israel, and anything my eyes behold is within my grasp if I but wish it.*

With a final glance at the comely woman, David descends from the roof and sends someone to find out about her. He discovers she is Bathsheba — the wife of his battle comrade, Uriah the Hittite.

David sends messengers to bring Bathsheba to the palace. She comes to him and lies with her. Then she returns home. Bathsheba conceives and sends word to the king of her pregnancy.

Uriah, Bathsheba's husband, was one of David's original mighty men. Part of the inner circle. One of his closest associates during the period of exile when loyalty meant everything. Yet, David plots to betray him.

The king calls Uriah to the palace and tells him he can go home to his wife. But Uriah is too faithful to the other soldiers to enjoy such luxury while they slept on the stony ground. Instead, he sleeps in the entrance to the palace with all his master's servants.

In the morning David asks him, "Why didn't you go home?"

"The ark and Israel and Judah are staying in tents, and my master Joab and my Lord's men are camped in the open fields," Uriah answers. "How could I go home to eat and drink and lie with my wife? As surely as you live, I will not do such a thing!"

Instead of rewarding such loyalty, David secretly orders Joab to put Uriah on the front line of battle where he will surely be killed. The troop commander does as he is ordered, and Uriah is killed by the strongest defenders of the city. After Bathsheba's period of mourning, David takes her as his wife.

Some of you reading this may find yourselves, like David, drawn to the delights of the eyes. Your "Bathsheba" may be money, prestige or a desperate climb up the corporate ladder of success. Or maybe yours is a stack of pornography hidden under the bed, an adulterous relationship, or a secret substance addiction.

Every man struggles with sin. But God says darkness and light have no relationship (1 John 1:5). When you begin to hide portions of your life in the darkness, to keep secrets, to protect yourself from the real truth of your sins — like David did — you are fighting a losing battle with the dark prince of this world.

David and his warriors conquered because they had extraordinary love for each other and did not abandon one another in the heat of battle. When David disassociated himself from his warriors, he began to commit sins that greatly saddened God. David committed adultery and murder! But God also was angry at David because he had betrayed one of God's loyal followers — and one of David's brothers in battle and in faith. He broke the code. He dishonored himself, Bathsheba, and God. He shattered the unity of the warriors.

Although David received support from many wives during his lifetime, he drew immense strength as a warrior for God from his close relationships with the other men who were also striving to do God's will. Modern men need these same relationships if they are to fight the good fight. Indeed, there is strength in numbers! (Taken from *Heart of the Warrior*, pp. 19-21.)

It's interesting to note that in one particular place in the Old Testament when it lists the sins of David it records "the betrayal of Uriah the Hittite" and not adultery with Bathsheba. You see, it's my belief that betrayal of one's brothers becomes the license for other sins to enter the camp — sins designed to destroy the unity of the warriors.

Men committing adultery begins when we as a masculine community have little or no regard for another man's wife, or our own wife, or ourselves and the God we serve. Most, if not all, identified "sins against humanity" are really a by-product of a lack of love for our fellow man. In the final analysis, the words of Nathan the Prophet to King David is to be a warning to us all:

> Why did you despise the word of the Lord by doing what is evil in his eyes? You struck down Uriah the Hittite with the sword and took his wife to be your

own. You killed him with the sword of the Ammonites. . . . This is what the Lord says: "Out of your own household I am going to bring calamity upon you. . . . You did it in secret, but I will do this thing in broad daylight before all Israel" (2 Sam. 12:9-12).

What we need to do to offset this sinful behavior and preserve the dignity of our homes is bring everything out of the darkness into God's wonderful light. We're talking about the hard work of accountability and confession where we vow to God in the company of Christian men: "NO MORE SECRETS AND NO MORE GOING IT ALONE." There is great truth to the old saying, "Temptation plus isolation often produces sin." Let's read about one man's spiritual journey from a hidden life of sin to the sanctifying work of the Holy Spirit.

A father with a young son was in prayer one day and felt compelled to go to another man to ask him to pray with him. He felt powerless to achieve his dreams and goals without the other man's help. As he began to share his weaknesses, an immediate bond formed between the men. His confessions were superficial at first, but convicted by the Spirit, he began to allow himself to become vulnerable. The friend knew of another man who should join them for their weekly prayer time, so the two quickly became three.

They met every Tuesday without fail to be an encouragement in prayer to one another, to lift up their burdens, and to claim the blessing that comes when two or three gather together in Christ's name. But, as the original father said, God had in mind a whole lot more.

"Although some things did change in our lives as we prayed, many did not," he confided. "It quickly became apparent that we would have to confess our sins to God — but in the company of each other. It seemed that somehow, unconfessed sin — sin that was repressed and denied — had power to blackmail us, to keep us in the darkness with a secret life that was hidden from the world. In a great many ways, we were pretending to be something we weren't."

The young dad said that even in private prayer, the men sometimes talked about their sins with God, but never truly confessed them — never laid them at God's feet. They would discuss worry or guilt about their general sinfulness, but they had difficulty admitting that they committed specific sins — and naming them. They all soon learned that God doesn't forgive the bad feelings that sin produces; he forgives sin.

"So we had to do the harder work of confessing sin for what it was," the young prayer partner said. "In the company of Christian friends, one brother's prayer of confession became what every other man needed. It broke the ice. When one brother confessed sin, the other two would hold him if he wept and encourage him when he needed it. This was strange stuff for us! But this unusual show of concern ushered in the blessing of God's forgiveness and offered hope to the two men who had yet to open up. As our confessional times became more open and trusting, we discovered we could confess sins, weep openly, and still be accepted as masculine in the company of men we knew and trusted."

As each brother confessed problems and sins in his life, he was drawn closer into the community of prayer warriors — strong, powerful men who had never before wept. Who had never before felt the love of deep fellowship and true camaraderie with other men. They weren't on a playing field. They were not at war. Yet, they discovered, it was OK, it was masculine, to talk and show genuine concern — even to hug and weep before the Lord.

"We felt a bond," the father said. "We moved from being impersonal, detached individuals to spiritual warriors. We each attacked the sins of our youth — everything from substance addictions and abuse of pornography to violent tempers and angry talk that hurt our wives and children. It was as though we actually engaged in battle against the old enemies of our fathers — those sinful habits that had been passed on to us through negative role-modeling and that we in turn would pass on to our children if we did not overcome them.

When King David was dying he called his son Solomon to him and told him to kill off his old enemies — enemies David should have killed, but failed to as he weakened in his old age. David's tolerance of such enemies was leading to horrible sins among his men as they began to betray and murder one another.

In the same way, the modern-day prayer brothers discovered that they often kept sins — those old enemies — in their lives, knowing full well that God wanted them to fight their way free of them.

"When those old enemies had been passed on to us, we hid them in the darkest parts of our worlds," the father recalled. "And so, our enemies continued to hold us in bondage; and as they did to our fathers before us, kept us spiritually weak."

The young men felt they had a form of godliness, but those old enemies hidden in their lives kept them from truly living out their Christianity.

In their prayers, the small group of men began to ask God to help them beat specific sins. With his strength, they began to crush them, one by one — low self-esteem, insufferable feelings of unworthiness, insecurity, sexual sin, chemical addiction and the like.

The young dad described the great feeling of relief he experienced when he and his two friends prayed together: "It was as if two older brothers were assembled with me, picking out my old enemies on the playground of life. As I stood in the protection of these strong brothers, I could watch as those intergenerational bullies fled in terror. We all felt deliverance like none we had ever known — and our lives began to change. It was remarkable."

As the men continued to meet, they left no stone unturned. They continued to delve into every nook and cranny of their lives, searching for sin like warriors with bright spotlights seeking all the hidden remnant in a conquered land. God's forgiveness covered them with peace — not because of some perfect confessional technique, but because God's grace is greater than any sin. He answered their prayers, and responded to their spirit of repentance.

Sometimes their prayers dealt with their marriages and their inability to properly love their wives.

"The old enemies of our fathers and the sins of our youth had haunted us and kept us from being the husbands we needed to be," one young man said, "and so those sins needed to be drawn and quartered, crushed, pulverized — destroyed like the others so they, too, no longer had any power over us. Once loosed, I felt the freedom to love as I had never loved before, as if a ball and chain were gone and I could glide effortlessly to the wife of my youth and make her needs mine."

Sexual addiction was in their way, the prayer brothers confessed.

"The beauty of our wives was lost amidst the lies of pornographic manipulation," they explained. "It caused us to believe the falsehood that the grass is greener anywhere else but at home. It caused us to believe that our sexuality wasn't being fulfilled, suggesting that we needed something more than our wives could provide. Now, with the enemy gone, our wives looked lovelier to us than ever. We were touched once again by those things that drew us to them in the beginning.

"With the enemy in full retreat, we could again see our wives as Jesus sees them: brides without spot or blemish. Again we saw their moral loveliness, and we found them infinitely worth embracing. With the enemy gone, we could remember what we had forgotten: 'They are the daughters of our King. They are princesses, royalty, bought with a price and sanctified with the blood of our Lord.' We fell in love with them all over again."

The dad also recalled his lack of involvement with his

son. He said it was as if he had been blind, deaf, mute and crippled — the very congenital diseases that Jesus chose to heal first — anomalies passed on from former generations. From father to son. "I was blind because I couldn't see my son's needs. I was deaf because I couldn't hear his cries for attention. I was mute — I couldn't speak the words of love he so longed to hear. And I was an invalid as far as his needs were concerned. I wasn't where he needed me to be — whether it was a ballgame or his PTA program," the young dad confessed.

But in the company of godly, praying men, the healing power of Jesus was unleashed again and whatever spiritual disease that had hampered the father began to leave. He was able to say, "I love you," for the first time, to listen to his son's heart as well as his words. He was there when his son needed him. And, most of all, he saw his son with new eyes — no longer as a burden, but as a blessing; a treasure from God.

As we live out this last decade of the 20th century, spiritual warriors, like the men mentioned above, will come together to reclaim their families for God and begin rebuilding the wall of spiritual protection for their sons and daughters who will be the leaders of the 21st century. Yet they must not try to take the stand alone. Satan is clever and sly. As David discovered, a close-knit band of warriors — courageous in faith and mighty in spirit — is the best and strongest line of defense against the devil's temptations and snares.

And so, here is the military objective as the warriors unite: to create a spiritually-fortified family in the midst of a world that values pride over humility, power over servanthood, and greed over love.

The strategies for battle are not as simple as a list of "10 Fast and Easy Ways to Become a Better Dad." And many men are not aware that a battle is even necessary. They believe that a strong hand of discipline is enough, with a little love thrown in for good measure.

But the world today is a battleground. Satan wants our

children — the next generation of Christians — to be weak, without knowledge, without a spiritual fortress to shield them from his evil minions.

Children — even some from loving, seemingly stable homes — are falling into promiscuity, multiple marriages, drugs, alcoholism and other serious problems. Adults from troubled homes are passing their problems on to their kids in the forms of child abuse, parental neglect, and sexual permissiveness.

But as Christian men come together and unite to strengthen their hearts as warriors for God, they also will strengthen their families, their churches, and their world. (Taken from *Heart of the Warrior*, pp. 22-27.)

As we conclude this portion of our study, I have included some helpful exercises to aid you in the task of developing a battle plan against temptation (this wonderful diagram comes from *Discipleship Journal*, issue 72, 1992).

A BATTLE PLAN AGAINST TEMPTATION

1. Scripture describes many ways in which a Christian can avoid giving in to temptation. For each Scripture below, write down the method of winning over temptation, then give a practical example of how you might do this.

Scripture	Way to Fight	Example
Gen. 39:11-12		
Matt. 4:3-4		
Matt. 5:29-30		
Matt. 26:41		

Rom. 13:14

1 Cor. 7:2,5

1 Cor. 10:13
Heb. 2:18

Eph. 6:10-17

1 Tim. 6:9-10

Heb. 11:24-26

James 4:7

1 Pet. 5:8

2. Think of a temptation you are now facing. Choose two of the ways to fight from the chart above, and formulate a plan for implementing them in the coming week.

(Obviously, the above exercises are meant to be done on an individual basis. The small group study questions to come are meant to be reflected upon in the company of godly men.)

Reflecting on Study Three

1. Why do you think God spared David's life after he had committed adultery with Bathsheba? (Refer to 2 Sam. 12:13.) How does this complement what is said in 1 John 1:8:10?

2. How is Nathan's reproach of David different from how we sometimes approach a brother caught up in sin? (Refer to 2 Sam. 12:1-7.) What can we learn from Nathan's style of reproach and how does it compare to Paul's counsel in 1 Timothy 5:1 or Galatians 6:1?

3. What are the obstacles that keep you from confessing sin to God in the company of brothers you can trust?

4. What are some of the "old enemies" of your father that need to be "drawn and quartered"?

5. What does the Bible mean when it says the sins of the fathers are visited upon the next generation?

6. What does 1 Corinthians 10:13 say to those who think they are the only ones who struggle with certain sins?

7. Why is a vow of confidentiality — "What we say here, stays here!" — an indispensable part of small group accountability?

8. Hebrews tells us that Jesus "was tempted in every way, just as we are — yet was without sin" (4:15). Are these words an encouragement to you? Why?

9. In Proverbs 25:28 it says, "A weak person is like a city broken into and left without walls." What do you think that means? What is its relevancy to you?

10. Discuss the following questions used in small group accountability:

A. Have you been with a woman anywhere this past week that might be seen as compromising?

B. Have any of your financial dealings lacked integrity?

C. Have you exposed yourself to any sexually explicit material?

D. Have you spent adequate time in Bible study and prayer?

E. Have you given priority time to your family?

F. Have you fulfilled the mandate of your calling?

G. Have you just lied to me?

Study Four
Forging A Warrior's Heart

This is perhaps *the* most important chapter in our eight-part study. Take your time and, if need be, read over the material more than once. What I am about to share with you is not new, just arranged a little differently for easier understanding. Primarily, we will deal with just three concepts that help develop the spiritual man and form the heart of the warrior. I consider this a critical lesson because it acknowledges that all *real* and *lasting* change in a man's life comes from God.

God, as both the author and perfector of our faith (see Heb. 12:2), wants a relationship with you. It's that simple. When we draw closer to him we draw closer to the possibility of being the kind of man we've always wanted to be. Neither this book nor some 10-step, how-to program will ever give you the fundamental ability to be all that you can be.

To coin an old phrase, "the answer isn't a plan, it's the man." And that man is Jesus Christ! It is on him, and no one else, we are to "fix our eyes" (Heb. 12:2).

We must continually remind ourselves: God sent Jesus

into the world to reconcile us to himself (see 2 Cor. 5:18-19). And by the blood of Jesus, and by the power of his resurrection, we are adopted into God's family as his sons (see Eph. 1:5). And as sons we now have a song even the angels cannot sing — a song about our new found relationship with the heavenly Father. This love song is what David and his mighty men wrote about in the Psalms. Let's think about it for a moment.

The same mighty men who were once isolated, alone, and filled with bitterness were now so transformed by the presence of God in their midst they began to shout aloud a new song and usher in the greatest age of worship the Hebrew world had ever known (see Ps. 40:3; 96:1; 149:1).

Remember what it was like to be in love?

Think back to the early days of your courtship with your wife or girlfriend. How you longed for her. How you wanted to spend all your time with her. And the phone bills — who can forget the phone bills? You just couldn't get enough of each other! Well, that's what being in love is supposed to be like — irrational, spontaneous, and completely devoted.

Even David spoke of his devotion to God in very romantic terms — hardly the language you'd expect from a warrior. (See Ps. 98:3; 100; 101:1 for examples.) But that's what happens when you hang out with God.

However, the problem is that so many of us men have settled for religion without God. Thus, we have ended up with faith without fruit, hope without Him, and love without life.

And now it's time to go back to the basics. To sit at the feet of the Master once again and remember just two, clear, and concise commandments of God that affect the heart, not just our minds, and move us from religiosity into a vibrant, growing spirituality with him.

Concept Number One: "A little bit of knowledge, when properly understood, can be powerfully applied."

Many men have lots of knowledge. We are in a democratic republic that places a great deal of emphasis on education. As a professor, I know what I'm talking about. Unfortunately, we understand so little of the knowledge we possess that we often apply even less. This is the same boat the Pharisees found themselves in. So much so that Jesus warned their converts to do as they say, but not as they do. (See Matt. 23:3.)

How many of us — as husbands or fathers — have been guilty of the same thing? Do we practice what we preach? Can we say like Paul, "Therefore I urge you to imitate me" (1 Cor. 4:16)? This is not unlike the language we find in Hebrews, where we are exhorted to remember our leaders and "imitate their faith" (13:7). Do we have a faith worthy of being imitated?

To correct this problem, Jesus changes the volume and scope of our search. Rather than seeking a lot of knowledge about God, he says settle for just a little to help you know him better. Then, take the little that you know about God (his ways versus our ways) and put it into practice everyday. The ability to apply it will come from God — with his fruit or character as an evidence of God's glory in you!

Here's the biblical context for our discussion.

In Matthew 22:34-40 Jesus is confronted by the Pharisees, who test him with the question, "Which is the greatest commandment in the law?" Jesus replied, "Love the Lord your God with all your heart and with all your soul and with all your might. . . . And . . . your neighbor as yourself. All the law and the prophets hang on these two commandments."

Here Jesus is saying you can either have all the law and the prophets — we're talking a lot of knowledge — or obey just two, clear, and concise commands of God. It's your choice. The one commandment of God or the many commandments of the Pharisees. Jesus might well have asked them, "If memorizing, analyzing, and theologizing all the law and the Prophets changes your life — then great! But if not, what difference does it make?"

The problem, however, was that for all of their study in the Word they never found God. (See John 5:39-40.) Oh, to be sure, they had a lot of *knowledge of God*, but they didn't *know God*. That's why they didn't know Jesus! They didn't recognize that he was God, too, because they were not in a loving relationship with the Almighty. Because they were not in a loving relationship with the Almighty, they were not in a loving relationship with anyone else — that's why their religiosity was so despised by the non-Jewish world.

The difference here, is that spirituality is built on knowing Christ and religiosity is built on mere "arguments and pretense" about the purposes of God. (Read 2 Cor. 10:5.) You see, when one is religious, he goes to the Word only to debate and to win petty tiffs — to prove or test how right or righteous he is. By contrast, those who are spiritual go to the Word only to see Jesus and to be convicted of their need for God's grace. In short, a religious man will search the Scriptures for *meaning*; a spiritual man will search the Scriptures for *God*.

Another example of God reversing the volume and scope of our search is found in the beginning of time, with Adam and Eve. Just as we do today, they had a choice between one, clear, and concise commandment of God or the many commandments of Eve.

Turn to Genesis 3:1-3 and I'll show you what I'm talking about. Here, Satan questions Eve about God's commandment to them. Hearing that she had *added* to God's Word, as the Pharisees would eventually do, Satan is able to lead her astray. Let's think about what *God actually said* versus what *Eve told the serpent.*

> **God said, "You must not eat from the tree of the knowledge of good and evil, for when you eat of it you will surely die" (Gen. 2:17).**
>
> **Eve said, "You must not eat fruit from the tree that is in the middle of the garden, *and you must not touch it,* or you will die" (Gen. 3:3, italics added).**

You see, God's one commandment is clear and concise: "You must not eat from the tree of the knowledge of good and evil." Eve's additional commandment is totally unnecessary: "You must not eat . . . you must not touch." So why, then, would Eve do such a thing? Because Eve reasons that if she touches the fruit she will eat it. But what happens when her additional prohibition doesn't work? Well, she has to either give in to temptation — which she eventually did — or keep adding new laws.

To drive home this point, let's see where Eve's legalistic mindset takes us. When she discovers that by not touching the fruit her temptation doesn't go away, she adds another commandment. This time it reads, "Thou shalt not get within a 50-mile radius of the wall." When that doesn't work, she adds another, "Thou shalt not get on the island with the knowledge of good and evil." When that doesn't work, then another, "Thou shalt not get within a 50-mile radius of the waters surrounding the island." Where does it all end? Well, that's the point — it doesn't! It just keeps on going and going and going — like the Energizer Bunny on T.V.

What Adam and Eve failed to understand is that it would be a loving relationship with God and not some man-made rules and regulations that would keep us from the penalty of sin. When we are able to have a righteousness of our own, by having the pretense of keeping the traditions of men perfectly, we tell the world — as Eve told the serpent — we don't need God. We can do it on our own. The truth, of course, is that we can't. And when we can't live up to the law, we break it secretly — as the Pharisees were doing — and pretend to be something we're not!

If Adam and Eve had simply admitted they were incapable of keeping God's one, clear, and concise commandment, and sought his forgiveness instead, then God's wonderful grace would have been available even then. Why, just think, expulsion from the garden might never have been necessary! As Paul teaches us, law reveals our sinfulness and our ultimate need for a Savior! (See Rom. 7:7-25.)

Concept Number Two: "We must move upward toward God, inward toward self, and then outward toward others."

We begin our discussion with Matthew 19:16-22. Here we have the account of the rich young ruler and his encounter with God. Notice that the man called Jesus "good teacher" (verse 16). Jesus asks, "Why do you call me good, there is only one who is good and that is God" (verse 17)? Here Jesus is appealing to the man's intellect. By Christ's logic, he sets the stage for the man to acknowledge who he is.

✢ Premise # 1: "Jesus is the *good* teacher."

✢ Premise # 2: "Only God is *good*."

✢ Conclusion: "Jesus is *God!*"

Forcing the rich young ruler to acknowledge that he was in the presence of God made the answer Jesus would give the man's question, "what must I do to get eternal life?" completely binding. Jesus was in essence issuing a warning, "Look, be careful what you ask for. I am not just some enlightened guru. Or just another rabbi. I am God. And the only way to get eternal life is through me."

But, knowing the man's heart, Jesus continues, "If you want to enter life, obey the commandments" (verse 17). And then, accommodating the rich young ruler, he lists them, "Do not murder, do not commit adultery, do not steal, do not give false testimony, honor your mother and father, and love your neighbor as yourself" (verse 18).

The man is pleased because he has kept all of them, he says. Hoping to settle his account with God once and for all, he asks, "What do I still lack" (verse 20)? Jesus answers — you lack God! Therefore, "Sell your possessions. . . . Then come follow me" (verse 21).

Now, look back at the commandments the rich young ruler is proud in having kept. Where is the focus, I ask you? Upward toward God, inward toward self, or outward toward others? I think if you study the list carefully you'll see that they all point *outwardly*.

The lesson of the rich young ruler is one we all should heed — being good enough is never good enough. It's not what we know, but who we know that makes all the difference in God's kingdom! Here, we have a man with self-righteousness. He has all the outward appearance of godliness, but a conspicuous absence of any real relationship with God. He is religious, but without God's spirit (see 1 Cor. 2:14). And according to Paul, such a man is not spiritual (see also 1 Cor. 2:1-16; 3:1-3), but worldly. Thus, the master physician Jesus prescribes individual heart surgery.

The bottom line is, we must first move upward in the direction of God. Ultimately, it will be a relationship with him through his Son, and nothing else, that will "strengthen you with power through his Spirit in your inner being so that Christ may dwell in your hearts through faith . . . that you . . . may have power, together with all the saints, to grasp how wide and long and high and deep is the love of Christ, and to know this love that surpasses knowledge — that you may be filled to the measure of all the fullness of God" (Eph. 3:16-19).

After we move upward, God's Holy Spirit takes us inward — to examine our inner being, says Paul — in God's attempt to convict us of wrongdoing. No longer desiring to live a secret life of repressed or denied sin, we can now freely confess our transgressions and affirm our need for Jesus who is "faithful and just," John tells us, and will "purify us from all unrighteousness" (1 John 1:9).

Such forgiveness — the experience of God's grace — moves us outwardly to love our neighbors as we have been loved! Thus, we fulfill God's greatest command by the redemptive power of the blood of the Lamb — Jesus.

Concept Number Three: "God sent the Holy Spirit to convict the world of sin, righteousness, and the judgment to come."

Our text is taken from John 16:5-11. "It is for your good that I am going away," Jesus tells his disciples. "Unless I go away, the Counselor will not come to you. . . . When he comes, he will convict the world of guilt in regard to sin . . . righteousness and judgment" (verses 7-8). On this occasion, Jesus is foretelling the sanctifying work of the Holy Spirit.

As men, husbands, and fathers, we must embrace this Counselor, too. We must allow him to come into our hearts and convict us of sin; that he might take it out and put righteousness in its place; so that we will escape the judgment of the world to come. What we experience, then, is what Paul writes about as life by the spirit:

> So I say, live by the Spirit, and you will not gratify the desires of the sinful nature. For the sinful nature desires what is contrary to the Spirit, and the Spirit what is contrary to the sinful nature. They are in conflict with each other, so that you do not do what you want. But if you are led by the Spirit, you are not under law.

> The acts of the sinful nature are obvious: sexual immorality, impurity and debauchery; idolatry and witchcraft; hatred, discord, jealousy, fits of rage, selfish ambition, dissensions, factions and envy; drunkenness, orgies, and the like. I warn you as I did before, that those who live like this will not inherit the kingdom of God.

> But the fruit of the Spirit is love, joy, peace, patience, kindness, faithfulness, gentleness and self-control. Against such things there is no law. Those who belong to Christ Jesus have crucified the sinful nature with its passions and desires. Since we live by the Spirit, let us keep in step with the Spirit (Gal. 5:16-25).

Now, I want you to study these two lists very carefully. Let's begin with the "acts of the sinful nature." These are the things that destroy a right relationship with God — sin alienates us from him (upwardly); and destroys a right relationship with self — we feel the guilt that sin produces (inwardly); and destroy a right relationship with our neighbor — when I commit adultery, it negatively affects my wife (outwardly). Are you starting to get the picture?

Conversely, the second list — "fruit of the Spirit" — promotes a right relationship with God, self, and others. It's just that simple! The more we hang out with God, and bask in his presence, the more he takes out of our lives those things that bring judgment — that is, produce destructive consequences. And, the more he puts his fruit or nature in its stead. We become more likable and easier to be around because we've become more like Jesus. Remember what our parents used to tell us, "You will be known by the company you keep." That's what being in the company of godly men — with Christ dwelling in your midst — is all about.

Paul the apostle didn't become a substitute for God, but he did what Jesus did: pointed to God. That's what the husband-father does for his family: he points them to God.

If you develop your own intimate relationship with God the Father, you can then boldly lead your family down that same path. Like John the Baptist, you can prepare the way for the Lord.

How do you become intimate with God? Through prayer and meditation on his word. How do you become closer to your wife and children? By praying with them and for them — every day.

Simply being in the presence of God will change you. Through his Holy Spirit, he will impact your masculinity. He will impact your daily life. How? No one knows. But the men who are experiencing it say they don't even care how anymore — they just know it works and it is making their relationships with their wives and children better than ever before.

Your marriage will change because you do this. Not because you go to a seminar. Not because you read 50 books. But because you've become something more than a religious man — a truly spiritual one. And because you point yourself and your family every day in God's direction.

God will change you. After all, God raised Jesus from the dead, totally unassisted by him. God has the power of the resurrection. And he can raise you and your family up with that same power through prayer and his Holy Spirit.

The Lord is calling you to do this. Your family needs you, mighty warrior, so put on the armor of God — starting today! (Taken from *Heart of the Warrior*, pp. 37-38.)

Reflecting on Study Four

1. What is the significance of John 5:39 to our lesson?

2. Read 2 Corinthians 11:3. What is Paul's concern here? How is it possible to be "led astray from the simplicity and purity of devotion to Christ"?

3. Do you agree with the following comment: "Jesus did not come to give us his knowledge, but to give us his mind"? What's the difference between "knowledge" and "mind"? Read aloud Philippians 2:1-11.

4. Do you agree with the premise, "The counterfeit of the mind of Christ is knowledge of religion — the counterfeit affects the head and the genuine affects the heart"? Why or why not?

5. Read Ecclesiastes 12:13. How is this complementary to Jesus' response to the Pharisees in Matthew 22:37?

6. Would you describe the home you were raised in as religious or spiritual? Explain.

7. Read Acts 5:1-11 and discuss whether or not "The Ananias and Sapphira Complex" — that is, lying to God — is still occurring today. How does this relate to Paul's category of sin, "selfish ambition" — that is, "to court popular applause through trickery," in Galatians 5:20?

8. Do you think concept number one — knowledge, understanding, and application — is valid? Why or why not?

9. Do you think concept number two — upward, inward, and outward — is a good framework for understanding Christianity in our homes, churches, and communities? Why or why not?

10. Some believe that merely focusing on "getting saved" has produced a psychological generation of men for whom there is no gospel for behavior and discipline, no sanctification process, and no confession and accountability. Would you agree? Tell the group why, and be very specific.

Study Five
Building Your Confidence as a Spiritual Warrior

Rob wants to be the spiritual leader of his home. He wants to tell his wife how he sees the need for more prayer and Bible study.

But Rob feels he's not worthy of the job.

His wife has seen him drunk. She has heard foul language come out of his mouth, occasionally directed at her. She knows that he slept with two women after their marriage.

Rob wants to tell her about his new spiritual awakening, but all of his failures burden his heart and make him afraid to speak the words. Such vulnerability, to open up to his wife that way! Such responsibility, once the words are spoken!

Rob's personal prayer life is in shambles, too. He knows he really needs her support to keep the sort of prayer life God wants. But would he get that support?

Remaining silent, Rob feels he has once again failed his family and his God.

In talking with this young man about becoming a spiritual leader of his home, it's easy to see his willingness — and that his embarrassment and fear are far greater. (Taken from *Heart of the Warrior*, pp. 39-40.)

No doubt, like Rob, you have felt the same way! You want to begin leading your home, but often feel like your wife is more spiritual than you. And maybe she is — that can be a blessing, in fact. A spiritual woman will give you the time it takes for God to change you. A spiritual woman knows that it's God and not nagging that will give her the man of her dreams. Trust me on this one, I've been there before.

But maybe you come from a home where your wife is not spiritual and her support for your role as the head of the family is on the decline. My recommendation is to ask her to read Study Three of this book and have her consult the Appendix of *Heart of the Warrior* for the article by Michelle Morris, "A Word to Wives." This will help her to understand your desire to be more like Christ and to lead as a shepherd with the father heart of God — lovingly and gently.

Part of resolving the ambivalence you feel is to forgive yourself by accepting that God, through Christ, has forgiven you.

> Regardless of how unworthy you feel to take on the duties of spiritual leader of your home, God can change all that.
>
> If you feel that past or present sin would make your prayers and new role in your family tantamount to hypocrisy, consider Romans 5:20, which tells us "where sin increased, grace increased all the more." First John 1:9 is likewise an inspiration, advising us, "If we confess our sins, he is faithful and just and will purify us from all unrighteousness."
>
> Throughout the book of Romans, Paul describes his change from a violent and quick-tempered man who lived in sin to a man of God whom many regarded as a spiritual father. He was changed through Christ! He was changed completely because he was willing to sub-

mit his old self, his powerful yet sinful self, to Christ to be changed into a new man.

Why is this change so important? Proverbs 14:12 explains, "There is a way that seems right to a man, but in the end it leads to death." God will awaken your spiritual sensibilities. You will see and hear God's Word differently. And now seeing and hearing, perhaps for the first time, you will be open to the possibility of change.

No one can define or describe what changes will take place in you. This depends on your own spiritual state and on your present struggles within yourself and your family.

Those who have begun to experience these changes can't quite put into words how God does it, but they will tell you, "I feel more masculine than ever before! I feel spiritually strong! I feel like the lover of my family, the leader of my home." These men are not super-religious saints who understand the Bible forward and backward. They may not even be men who have had any sort of regular prayer life in the past.

In fact, the men who have begun to rediscover biblical masculinity and spiritual leadership also discover that they now know their weaknesses better than ever — and accept them. They turn these weaknesses over to God instead of continuing to fight these battles inside themselves. These men share their weaknesses with their wives and prayer partners and receive their support as they work with God to overcome the difficulties.

But one thing is sure: their fear was just as strong as any man's. The difference is that they chose to take a step of faith with God and allowed him to begin changing them and their families. The results are amazing! (Taken from *Heart of the Warrior*, pp. 42-43.)

Taking a step of faith with God will build your confidence as a spiritual warrior. To grasp how, one needs to understand the difference between *religious faith* and *spiritual faith*.

According to Randy Stephens, a gifted teacher and friend, when a man speaks of faith, he's really talking about a system of belief he's inherited from his family of origin — such as, Methodism, Lutheranism, or Catholicism, for example — or a set of doctrinal issues, like the Nicene Creed, that often might not affect his heart or actions. Randy goes on to say that religious faith is intellectual (affecting only the head) and largely without action. Seen from this standpoint, then, "A strong and accurate faith is no different from a weak and inaccurate faith." I agree with Randy.

Spiritual faith, by contrast, is supernatural (affecting the heart) and always includes action. Let's consider the second chapter of James, where the Lord's brother draws a fine line between religious faith and spiritual faith. Here, James — particularly in verses 14 and 26 of our text — demonstrates a correlation between faith and action, and even goes on to write that "faith without deeds is dead."

To understand further the dynamics of faith, we must go to Hebrews chapter eleven.

Verse one is quoted many times as the definition of faith — often without recognizing the full or greater impact of this verse. One way to get a better handle on what is being said here is to go back to chapter one of Hebrews and examine verse three. There you will find the words "the exact representation" referring to Jesus Christ. The Greek words here are used interchangeably with the words "being sure" in chapter eleven verse one.

Now, let's reexamine verse one in light of this interchange: "Faith is *the exact representation* of what we hope for and the certainty of what we do not see." The clarification here tells me that my faith is exactly represented by my hope.

"Whatever actions we perform," says Randy Stephens, "whether others see them or just you and God know about them, is your faith and your hope. In other words, your life is your faith. Faith is not possessed as knowledge is possessed — your faith is your walk, whether it is Christlike or not! Seen from this view, everyone has faith. By observing those things that someone's life strives for, we can determine what their faith is in."

Casual reading of the rest of the chapter clearly illustrates the idea of our faith, our hope, being combined with action:

✧ Abel *offered* (action) — verse 4

✧ Noah *built* (action) — verse 7

✧ Abraham *went* (action) — verse 8

✧ Abraham *prepared* to sacrifice (action) — verse 17

✧ Isaac and Jacob *blessed* (action) — verses 20-21

✧ Joseph *spoke* (action) — verse 22

✧ Moses' parents *hid* (action) — verse 23

✧ Moses *left* (action) — verse 27

✧ The people *passed* (action) — verse 29

✧ People *marched* (action) — verse 30

If my faith is in education, then my hope will be exactly represented by my faith. That is to say, my hope will be to become more educated or to acquire more knowledge. Therefore, I should be more educated or knowledgeable today than I was this same time last year — even though I couldn't see it!

If, on the other hand, my faith is in Jesus, then my hope will be to become more like him. Now, accountability becomes easier because my faith focus is *spiritual* rather than *religious*. So that today I am potentially more like Christ than I was this same time last year — even though I couldn't see, or even at times comprehend, how or in what ways God would do this. This is taking a step of faith with God!

Notice how in God's "Hall of Faith" as listed above, spiritual faith involves the certainty of things unseen. Consider the following:

 ✧ Our visible universe was spoken into existence from nothing — verse 2

 ✧ Abel offered the better sacrifice, before seeing God's approval — verse 4

 ✧ For 120 years, Noah prepared for rain — something never seen before — verse 7

 ✧ Abraham began a journey to a place he had never seen before — verse 8

 ✧ Abraham believed God would raise his son from the dead, although he never saw such an occurrence, because of God's promise — verse 19

 ✧ Joseph knew his people would leave Egypt and left instructions concerning his body — verse 22

 ✧ The entire exodus story is laced with the "unseen." The "destroyer of the firstborn" was feared, but had never been seen. The people walked between two walls of water, never having seen water stand without physical, tangible restraint for more than a fraction of a second — verses 24-29

 ✧ The people obeyed, not knowing how victory would be secured — verse 30

The conclusion, says Stephens: "God's word is certain.

Whether we understand the why's or the wherefore's of the commands that we learn, a spiritual faith will act on the command."

Your wife may be hesitant at first to trust your spiritual leadership if she has held the reins for some time. But if you begin to show her that you want to be the chief servant in a family of servants, that you are seeking to be a Spirit-controlled man, her love and respect for you can only increase.

For many, this will be no small change. It will be monumental. Many men have been the person they are for 20, 30, even 50 or more years and are afraid of losing themselves.

So many of us may be thinking, "Sure I'm not perfect. I'm not particularly attached to any of my sins . . . but if I turn my whole life over to God, what happens to me? Who will I be?" We're afraid we won't recognize the "new creation" that God will produce in our lives.

According to the Bible, this attitude is common to all men and women. But this fear of losing "self" can be overcome through God. In Romans 12:1, Paul writes, ". . . present your bodies as living sacrifices, holy and pleasing to God — this is you spiritual act of worship."

Those words may be easy enough to read and maybe even easy to understand with our minds, but they are more difficult to bring into our hearts.

Part of the problem is that although we want to present our bodies as living sacrifices — somehow we wind up crawling off the altar instead. The thought of dying to self is frightening. It's a scary proposition to realize we should put the will of God and the needs of our wives and children above our own desires and needs.

Dare I ask what God wants and commit myself to meeting his expectations? And my wife — what if I can't comply with her needs? you may ask yourself.

But when a man dies to himself daily and lives for God and his family, his true self emerges — his God-created image is restored! Seeing and hearing with the eyes and ears of a man created in the image of God, maturity is unleashed, and according to Paul, he is able to finally put away childish things ("the sins of youth," 2 Tim. 2:22) and begin to speak and act like a man (1 Cor. 13:11).

These changes will not be easy, but the need is absolute and immediate. You must find the courage to begin today, remembering the hopeful words of Paul to the saints in Philippi: "I can do everything through him who gives me strength" (Phil. 4:13). (Taken from *Heart of the Warrior*, pp. 46-47.)

Reflecting on Study Five

1. In Galatians 5:5, Paul states, "By faith we eagerly await through the Spirit the righteousness for which we hope." What do you think Paul is saying here, and how does it apply to you and me?

2. Could the word "righteousness" be another term for our singular hope?

3. Romans 12:9-12 records that, as Christian men and brothers, we should have "sincere love," "joyful hope," and "prayers of faith." Consider each category and relate them to what you have learned so far. (Note: "sincere" means transparent — what you see is what you get, etc. The other adjectives should be more obvious.)

4. Read the following passages of Scripture aloud:
    - Galatians 5:5-6
    - Ephesians 4:2-6
    - Colossians 1:4-5
    - 1 Thessalonians 1:3
    - 1 Thessalonians 5:8
    - Hebrews 6:10-12
    - Hebrews 10:19-25
    - 1 Peter 1:3-9; 21-22

    What do all these passages have in common?

5. Do you agree with the following statement from Randy Stephens: "If I seek to over-complicate God's

61

truth, my Christianity will turn into a sterile belief system, resembling a vain religious philosophy rather than a powerful, pure, and holy life that brings glory to God"? Why or why not?

6. Read Luke 6:46 aloud. What's the warning here and how does it relate to what we have just learned about faith?

7. Would you agree that our ability to obey God — that is, do the things he has commanded — comes out of our relationship with Jesus Christ? Explain.

8. Would you agree that a personal relationship with God based on faith, hope, and love brings forth life; but an intellectual, detached relationship with God based merely on knowledge brings forth death? Explain.

9. Read aloud 2 Corinthians 3:3-6. What is the point of this passage?

10. Paul talks about being conformed to the likeness of Jesus Christ (Rom. 8:29). What significance is that to the spiritual warrior as head of his home?

Study Six
The Apprenticeship
of a Warrior

Many men in today's world of broken homes and mixed-up families did not even have a father present in their homes. They have no role model to follow, good or bad. Other men grew up with fathers who were too busy, too distant or just too unapproachable for their sons to ever draw close to them.

Therefore, grown men — now husbands and fathers themselves — often have a "surface" relationship with their dads. They may see each other regularly, help fix the car or repair the roof, maybe watch a game together — but they don't talk much.

The son doesn't ask the hard questions: Have you ever failed, Dad? How did you come to your faith, Dad? Are you ever tempted? Do you pray with Mom? Does life ever scare you? Do you ever feel God's love? Do you ever sin? How can I be a good Dad?

One man, now middle-aged, grew up with a dad who never touched him physically — in affection or punishment — but frequently told him what a failure he was when he did not live up to his dad's expectations. His father never praised, only criticized. The boy grew into a perfectionist who couldn't accept faults in anyone — particularly himself.

The man's father died. He knew he should grieve, but he couldn't. In fact, staring into his father's casket, he looked inside himself and found only relief.

Our world does not encourage men to be close. They touch more on a football field than they'd ever dream of touching in a non-sports setting. Men sometimes compliment each other's achievements, especially those related to work or athletics, but rarely give praise for successes as fathers or husbands.

Men talk comfortably about many subjects — as long as they don't relate to spirituality, weakness, relationships, or God. Christian men — especially our ministers, elders and other church leaders — often find it difficult to share spiritual weaknesses with anyone. The more godly people perceive them to be, the more men believe they must hide their weak spots.

This discomfort, preventing men from sharing and communicating, carries into the home and affects the relationship between fathers and sons. Spiritual matters may not be taboo, but questions about spirituality sometimes receive a lukewarm response from fathers who feel nervous about revealing too much of themselves.

And a dad who is uncomfortable serving as the spiritual leader of his home will raise children who are also afraid to take on their God-given responsibilities. Such a father may provide well for his wife and children but will not know how to develop an intimate relationship with the heavenly Father. Therefore, he'll also fail to develop such a relationship with his family. Intimacy with God births intimacy with others — and distance from him spawns distance in all other human relationships.

Before you can believe in your success as a husband and father, you've got to experience success as a son. And God is the *only* perfect Father.

But how can a man who has a damaged relationship with his earthly father develop intimacy with a God he has never seen? How can a man who has lost the opportunity to reconcile with his human father find a way to reconcile with the Father in heaven? If he could never be convinced of the acceptance of the man who sired him, how will he ever learn to trust the acceptance of the God who created him?

First of all, if your father is living, you have a special task. If you have difficulties in your relationship — even much pain and bitterness — God asks that you "forgive whatever grievances you may have against one another" (Col. 4:15).

Jesus himself convicts us in Mark 11:25, "And when you stand praying, if you hold anything against anyone, forgive him, so that your Father in heaven may forgive you your sins."

For some of you, this may be the most difficult thing you have ever done. For some men, the idea of God as a heavenly Father is impossible to comprehend because their fathers — or their lack of a father — caused them so much pain.

However, this important process of forgiveness begins with prayer. Lift up your father in prayer. Pray that your own heart be opened to him, that your eyes be opened to his struggles and weaknesses. Then pray for his heart to be softened and for his eyes to see your needs as his beloved son.

Even if your father is deceased, you may still hold much anger and bitterness toward him. Pray that your heart might be opened to the forgiveness God makes possible for you. What you have never been able to accomplish alone, God can do through his Spirit in you.

If your father abused you physically or emotionally, or if he abandoned you when you most needed him, such prayer may seem like bitter gall to you. Even if your father is an "ordinary Joe" Christian who simply failed to meet your spiritual needs, you may strongly resist the need for prayer that could lead to forgiveness.

But God calls you, men, to begin this reconciliation

process. If your father has passed away, if you never knew him, if he never responded to your attempts to reach out — you must still begin to forgive him in your heart.

You are not alone in your struggle. God will help you if you lift this burden up to him in prayer. As Jesus said in Mark 11:24, ". . . whatever you ask for in prayer, believe that you have received it, and it will be yours."

If you still have the opportunity to talk with your dad, God calls you to share your concerns with him. Tell him why you are angry or hurt or sad. Tell him how you hope to improve your relationship with him as you enhance your relationship with God the Father. He may or may not understand, but you will begin to find peace as you pray and work toward reconciliation.

You may believe you had a pretty healthy relationship with your father. Maybe he hugged you, told you he loved you, and praised you not only for your achievements but because you were his special son. Thank God for such a special father and leader in your home! Ask the heavenly Father to empower you to emulate such godly behavior in your own home.

The process of reconciling with your own father is important, but it is only the first step. In fact, for some of you, working on the relationship with your earthly father may be easier once you develop a closer relationship with God.

No matter what kind of relationship you had with your dad, the relationship you are developing with God will be more wonderful, more fulfilling and more enriching than you can even imagine.

Why is this relationship with God so important for fathers? Because if you are going to serve as your family's spiritual leader and protector from Satan's attacks, you must become closer to God — the giver of all strength and all peace. David wrote in Psalm 18:32, "It is God who gives me strength and makes my way perfect." But God expects something from you: your faithfulness and willingness to serve him. Second Chronicles 16:9 explains how the Father will bless you if you develop a closer relationship with him: "For the eyes of the Lord range throughout the earth to strengthen those whose hearts are fully committed to him." (Taken from *Heart of the Warrior*, pp. 51-55.)

So far we have concentrated our lesson on the healing of our masculine souls. Why? Because, before we can become fathers — spiritual warriors who are able to pass our weapons of warfare on to the next generation of sons and daughters — we have to first become sons. This begins with our earthly fathers, then with our heavenly one.

This is exactly what Jesus was saying to Nicodemus in John's Gospel, chapter three. "I tell you the truth, no one can see the kingdom of God unless he is *born again*" (verse 3, italics added). "How can a man be born when he is old?" Nicodemus asked. "Surely he cannot enter a second time into his mother's womb to be born" (verse 4).

Jesus answered, "I tell you the truth, no one can enter the kingdom of God unless he is born of water and the Spirit. *Flesh gives birth to flesh, but the Spirit gives birth to spirit*" (verses 5-6, italics added).

This is great news for us men whose earthly fathers fell short of our expectations. You see, God has not left us orphans! He comes that we might have life a second time — a Spirit-filled life. Just as the hymn rightfully proclaims, "He walks with me, and he talks with me, and he tells me I am his own."

God sent Jesus to die for us "that we might receive the full rights of sons. Because you are sons, God sent the Spirit of his Son into our hearts, the Spirit calls out, 'Abba, Father.' So you are no longer a slave, but a son; and since you are a son, God has made you also an heir" (Gal. 4:5-7).

We are heirs to God's eternal salvation. We are children of God, and as such he has given us the privilege of developing an intimate relationship with him. Galatians 3:26 says, "You are sons of God through faith in Jesus Christ, for all of you who were baptized into Christ have clothed yourself with Christ."

Men, we need not be timid or afraid in our faith as we begin a more godly walk before our families. Romans 8:15-16 tells us: "You did not receive a spirit that makes you a slave to fear, but you received the Spirit of Sonship. And by him we cry, 'Abba, Father.'"

Paul continues in Romans, "The Spirit himself testifies with our spirit that we are God's children. Now if we are children, then we are heirs — heirs of God and co-heirs with Christ."

Men, husbands, and fathers — if you have never felt fully accepted by your own father, if you still feel an emptiness that your dad did not fill — come to your heavenly Father. He has accepted you as his son if you have called him into you life as Savior and Lord.

God tells us that he has sent his Spirit "to help us in our weakness" (Rom. 8:26). The Bible tells us boldly, "If God is for us, who can be against us? He did not spare his own Son, but gave him up for us all — how will he not also, along with him, graciously give us all things?" (Rom. 8:31-32). (Taken from *Heart of the Warrior*, p. 59.)

Our apprenticeship as warriors now belongs with God, our Father. He calls us out from the world to experience his love and forgiveness. And then, he gives us his Spirit so that through sanctification we truly become like father, like son. "Be imitators of God," writes Paul, "as dearly loved children" (Eph. 5:1). That's what an apprentice does, he *imitates* his master. Paul affirms this when he instructs the early church to imitate him (see 1 Cor. 4:16). He then writes, "For this reason I am sending to you Timothy, my son whom I love, who is faithful in the Lord. He will remind you of my way of life in

Christ Jesus" (verse 17).

This tradition of raising up a leader for God's people through intense discipleship or apprenticeship has been lacking in the churches today. Oh, how God longs for a man of God, like Paul, to train and equip the future Timothys of the church. Many men now agree that each Christian — as a Timothy — needs a Paul; and every Christian —as a Paul — needs a Timothy!

It's like we've forgotten how to prepare the leaders of the 21st century. As though we no longer remember: CHRISTIANITY IS CAUGHT, NOT TAUGHT!

Older men used to speak powerfully into the lives of younger men by example and discipleship — largely the role of presbytery. The elders of the community felt it was their responsibility to call out the men from the boys and empower them to take up the mantle of manhood. They knew that the welfare of the community demanded it.

This process involved a kind of "Rites of Passage" — where the songs of the elders made mothers cry and boys men!

> Vertigo and smoke, carried on the haunting notes of sacred flutes fashioned from hollowed bamboo shafts, floated into the Belly of the Crocodile. Eleven adolescent males sat cross-legged in a semicircle on the wooden floor, their wounds glistening as they listened intently to the music. No longer boys but not yet men, they were in the midst of the manhood ritual of scarification, a month-long physical and mental ordeal designed to enlighten them with knowledge and courage, but also burden them with the responsibility of being men in the remote Papua New Guinea village of Kanganaman. Scars inflicted during the ceremony run the length of their bodies, representing wounds left by the teeth of a crocodile during an attack. The effect

is to make them men, with row after row of scalelike raised flesh, to resemble the reptile they both fear and revere.

Watbangu, a twenty-year-old initiate, leaned close and spoke in a low voice. The flutes were singing the Song of the Crocodile, he explained, signifying the joy the elders felt because the boys were becoming men. To the boys' biological mothers, the music symbolized the loss of sons who would no longer answer to women — mothers or otherwise. "Sometimes when our mothers hear the music, they cry," Watbangu whispered through the haze of three smoldering fires. "We have new mothers now." (Taken from "In the Belly of the Crocodile," *American Way*, p. 53, February 1, 1992.)

The Christian community needs to bring back a similar manhood ritual. One where fathers bring their adolescent sons to the elders of the church to lay hands on them and bless them — proclaiming them born again of the water and the Spirit! Oh, how powerful that would be. And how closely parallel to what Paul did for Timothy.

Timothy was a man of God who received his faith and his knowledge of God through his maternal lineage: his grandmother Lois and his mother Eunice (2 Tim. 1:5). In fact, the book of Acts explains that Timothy's father was Greek, not Hebrew — and was probably not equipped to teach Timothy what he would need to know about manhood in a Jewish community.

Because Timothy received his faith heritage from the women in his life, he never had a chance to observe his father acting as the spiritual leader for his family or serving as the conduit for the word of God in Timothy's life. Perhaps this is why Paul reminds Timothy that he should not portray a "spirit of timidity" (2 Tim. 1:7).

Although the exact ramifications of this spirit of timidity are not clearly delineated in Scripture, it seems possible that Timothy was struggling with a lack of a male spiritual role model in his life and the great insecurity that lack produced. Could this be why Paul "adopted" Timothy as his son, becoming his spiritual father (1 Tim. 1:2,18; 2 Tim. 1:2; 2:1)?

Paul reminds him to "fan into flame the gift of God," which was in Timothy through the laying on of the apostle Paul's hands (2 Tim. 1:6). Paul provided Timothy with a spiritual blessing from father to son — something Timothy may not have received from his own earthly father.

Paul tells Timothy in 2 Timothy 1:14 not to neglect the gift that was entrusted to him. He urges him to "guard it with the help of the Holy Spirit who lives in us."

Paul's instructions to Timothy often sound like a father's instructions to his son — to enable him, to empower him, and to pass to him the mantle of manhood. This becomes more obvious in 2 Timothy 2:22, when Paul tells Timothy, "Flee the evil desires of youth, and pursue righteousness, faith, love and peace, along with those who call on the Lord out of a pure heart."

In 1 Corinthians 13:11, Paul uses parallel language about young faith versus mature faith: "When I was a child, I talked like a child, I thought like a child, I reasoned like a child. When I became a man, I put childish ways behind me."

By adopting Timothy as a spiritual son, Paul is calling Timothy to embrace the full measure of his giftedness as a man. The possible implications of Timothy's story are rather extraordinary and far-reaching. (Taken from *Heart of the Warrior*, pp. 55-57.)

When Christ, our Lord, was baptized by John the Baptist, God's voice from heaven was heard to say, "You are my Son, whom I love; with you I am well pleased" (Luke 3:22). As warriors, we must capture with our hearts and from the lips of our heavenly Father the same prophetic proclamation that we are his beloved sons in whom he is well pleased!

Reflecting on Study Six

1. Would you agree that many young girls are getting involved in illicit sexual relationships with boys for nonsexual reasons? Could it be that they are really searching for the father they never had or didn't know quite well?

2. Research now demonstrates that the *more nurturing* the father the *less sexually promiscuous* the daughter; conversely, the *more nurturing* the father the *more masculine* the son. What's your reaction to these findings?

3. Do you agree with the statement, "As the father goes, so goes the family"? Why or why not? How about, "As the family goes, so goes the church"?

4. Go around the room, and one at a time, share a little about your father.

5. What in American culture distinguishes the men from the boys? Explain.

6. What is the concept of discipleship as you understand it and should it be restored to the church? Explain.

7. Discuss the difference, as you understand it, between positional authority and relational authority. Refer to Paul's relationship with Timothy.

8. Should every man have both a Paul and a Timothy in his life? Explain.

9. If you could create a Christian "Rites of Passage" for adolescent males (or for men who are new converts), what would it be?

10. Voluntarily, have the older men place the younger men in chairs one at a time, and laying their hands on each one pray — and if possible, sing — a blessing over them. Now have the older men sit in chairs in the middle of the room while the younger men honor them with prayers of thanksgiving and a clap offering on their behalf. Discuss how you feel.

Study Seven
Rediscovering Biblical
Masculinity

The now-famous manhood guru, Robert Bly, would have a man believe that to be truly masculine he should isolate himself somewhere, beat a drum, and let loose a primal scream. That he should search for that wild, natural masculine instinct that he's lost in the sea of feminism and domestication by females.

Bly does not, however, teach men how to take that supposedly natural, "masculine" instinct back into their homes to help them care for their children and love their wives.

Fortunately, neither Bly's nor society's definitions of masculinity are the final answers for men. In the Bible, God has clearly laid out desired traits in men as well as their responsibilities.

While sketching his portrait of the ideal elder and deacon for the church, Paul writes in 1 Timothy 3:4-5, "He must manage his own household well and see that his children obey him with proper respect. If anyone does not know how to manage his own family, how can he take care of God's church?" In the same chapter, he describes a worthy man as "not violent, but gentle, not quarrelsome, not a lover of money."

Later in 1 Timothy, Paul tells Timothy how to avoid the

griefs many experience because of greed: "But you, man of God, flee from all of this, and pursue righteousness, godliness, faith, love, endurance and gentleness. Fight the good fight of faith." Isn't that interesting? Paul tells Timothy to fight — by pursuing faith, love and gentleness! These are definitely not the battle tactics of the world. (Taken from *Heart of the Warrior*, pp. 63-64.)

What Paul is describing above are the heart qualifications for leadership in the home, church, and community. It is the development of the inner man, so that our masculine selves resemble Jesus — and not James Bond, Superman, or Rambo. And it is with these Christlike qualities — righteousness, godliness, faith, love, endurance, and gentleness — that we fight the good fight as true spiritual warriors of God.

To the Hebrews, the idea of a man's heart included a person's mental, physical, and spiritual life — in essence, the whole man. Taken from the word *labab*, it placed a man's real existence in the innermost or hidden parts of himself that only God could see. The Greek word *kardia* also refers to the core of a man's mental, physical, and spiritual life. It is this core that gives birth to the very expression of a man's character. Change the heart, and you change the man.

That's why when dealing with definitions of masculinity, one needs to consider the condition of the heart and not just what a guy looks like on the outside. Looks can be very deceiving!

We notice this when Samuel the prophet goes to anoint David to one day be king.

Not yet knowing that David is the one chosen by God, Samuel sees Jesse's son Eliab and says, "Surely the Lord's anointed stands before the Lord." Eliab was Samuel's idea of masculinity — tall, dark, and handsome. But God said to Samuel, "Do not consider his appearance or his height, for I have rejected him. The Lord does not look at the things man looks at. Man looks at the outward appearance, but the Lord looks at the heart" (1 Sam. 16:6-7).

The key here is that true biblical masculinity comes from the father heart of God. David was chosen as a leader over the house of Israel because he had a heart after God's own — that is, a heart that resembled the father heart of God! Where did David get such a heart? By the faithful obedience of his father, Jesse. David simply imitated him — his thoughts, passions, desires, appetites, affections, purposes, and endeavors.

You see, when a boy passes the rite of manhood it is expected that he will soon take a wife and father his own household, bringing up his children in the fear and instruction of the Lord. The man, as father, now takes his wisdom, knowledge, and understanding of the things of God and transmits it to his son by way of the father and son relationship. Consider Proverbs, that was written by David's son, Solomon, and reflects how David taught him:

✧ Listen my son, to your father's instruction (1:8)

✧ My son, if sinners entice you, do not give in to them (1:10)

✧ My son, if you accept my words and store up my commands within you (2:1)

✧ My son, do not forget my teaching (3:1)

✧ My son, pay attention to what I say (4:20)

True biblical masculinity is generative by nature — that is, it cares and nurtures the next generation. It acknowledges that, when all is said and done, the home — as headed by the father — is the principal laboratory for the passing on of life skills and faith development.

Let's go on to read about Jesus as our role model — that is, nurturer — of biblical masculinity:

> God gives Christian men a clear example of masculinity in the Bible: Jesus. Hebrews 1:3 states, "The Son is the exact representation of God's being, sustaining all things by his powerful word." Jesus is the kind of man God approves. He is the exact representation of God himself! And when Paul wants to describe for the Christians in Ephesus how married men should behave toward their wives, what example does he use? "Husbands, love your wives, *as Christ loved the church* and gave himself up for her . . ." (Eph. 5:25, italics added).

> Yet when Jesus walked the earth as a man, he was the exact opposite of what the world expected.

> They wanted a ruler;
>> he gave them a servant.

> They wanted a man of power;
>> he gave them a man of gentleness and humility.

> They wanted a man beyond worldly reproach;
>> he ate with sinners.

> They tried to send the children away from him;
>> he took the little ones in his arms
>> and blessed them.

> They wanted him to save them immediately
>> from earthly problems;
>> he gave up his life to save them for eternity.

> As it says in Philippians 2:5-8, "Jesus Christ, who being in very nature God, did not consider equality with God something to be grasped, but made himself nothing, taking the very nature of a servant, being made in human likeness. And being found in appearance as a man, he humbled himself and became obedient to death — even death on a cross!"

A king who serves. A Messiah who eats with sinners. A creator who becomes one of his creatures. A God who dies. Is it any surprise, then, that Jesus' example of masculinity is opposite of the world's definition?

Jesus was gentle and loving, yet willing to openly rebuke evil. He was slow to anger, yet he showed righteous anger when his Father's temple was defiled. He forgave easily, openly wept over the death of his friend, and went out of his way to show kindness to a small, sinful man named Zacchaeus.

Men today don't understand biblical masculinity, much as Peter did not understand Jesus' kingship. When Jesus was washing Peter's feet, Peter says, "No!" Perhaps he reasons, *This is not the way a king behaves. His origin is divine. This is not my idea of what a leader should do!* The response of Jesus? "If I don't serve you, you aren't one of my people!"

Peter showed at several other points in Jesus' ministry that he was having trouble understanding Jesus' concept of kingship. Peter was no wimp. He wanted to fight off all the soldiers who would take his Lord — he even cut one man's ear off!

Yet when Jesus was describing the ministry he wanted Peter to take up, he did not ask Peter to slaughter his sheep or herd them in or even to rule over them — he said, "Feed my sheep."

Western society relegates the task of feeding to women. When Jesus wanted to feed hundreds of people who were sitting on a hillside listening to his words, he could have told the disciples to gather all the women and have them serve the crowd. Instead, he instructed the male disciples to feed the crowd.

In one of his appearances after the resurrection, Jesus was sitting on the lake shore preparing breakfast for his disciples. He could have asked someone else to cook food for the men. But he served them himself.

Clearly, in Jesus' view, the leader is the one who serves.

Men today can identify with Peter's desire to fight for his king, to show strength through anger rather than through gentleness and a Spirit-controlled temperament. However, God calls men to a different lifestyle — one of service and love. "Get rid of all bitterness, rage and anger, brawling and slander, along with every form of malice. Be kind and compassionate to one another, forgiving each other, just as in Christ God forgave you. Be imitators of God, and live a life of love" (Eph. 4:31; 5:1).

The father is the chief servant in a family of servants. And Jesus set the example.

In Mark 10:42-45, Jesus describes biblical leadership in terms largely unfamiliar to our culture:

> You know that those who are regarded as rulers of the Gentiles rule it over them, and their high officials exercise authority over them. Not so with you. Instead, whoever wants to become great among you must be your servant, and whoever wants to be first must be the slave of all. For even the Son of Man did not come to be served, but to serve, and to give his life as a ransom for many.

Men must lead their wives and children by setting an example of servanthood in the home — servanthood characterized by acts of love. According to Keith Miller, "loving acts can be very powerful if they are specific." The actions do not have to be profound — just thoughtful.

One wife in her late 20s with two young children says she feels loved if her husband remembers the family is out of milk and stops to pick some up on his way home from work. She also feels extra special when he takes over her regular household responsibilities — in addition to his own — because he thinks she needs a break for a day. Her husband shows his love for their oldest daughter by taking her out on Saturday morning for a drive and breakfast — and he often tops off the day by returning with flowers for his wife.

Taken alone, none of these actions is earth-shattering. But taken together in an atmosphere of loving consideration, by these deeds this husband is forging a chain of godly love that Satan cannot break — a chain that binds him to his family; that binds his family to God. (Taken from *Heart of the Warrior*, pp. 64-67.)

Reflecting on Study Seven

1. Read aloud the following Scriptures and tell why they fly in the face of traditional definitions of masculinity:

  - 2 Timothy 2:24
  - Titus 3:2
  - James 3:17
  - 2 Corinthians 1:1
  - Galatians 5:22
  - 1 Thessalonians 2:7

2. Jesus was the chief servant and modeled for us the concept of servant-leadership as a very real part of his masculine identity. Explore the following Scriptures together:

  - Luke 12:37
  - Luke 22:27
  - Mark 10:43
  - John 12:24-26
  - Philippians 2:8

3. After having read John 13, voluntarily wash each other's feet. Discuss your feelings. (This will obviously take some forethought and planning.)

4. Read Malachi 1:2-3 where it says, "I have loved Jacob but I have hated Esau." What do you think God knew about Esau's heart versus Jacob's? (Consider also Genesis 32:24-32.)

5. Do you agree that true spiritual masculinity requires neither natural strength, athletic ability, nor intellectual prowess? Explain. (Read 2 Corinthians 12:9 and 1 Corinthians 1:27.)

6. Isaiah has a powerful prophecy regarding Christ's physical appearance as a man in 53:2. What is the significance of these Scriptures to men today?

7. Some are saying that in the latter half of the 20th century we have experienced the "feminization of the church." What do you think is meant by that phrase and do you agree or disagree?

8. What do the following Scriptures — Proverbs 4:23; Philippians 4:7 — say about guarding the heart? How do these two Scriptures relate to Matthew 12:34b-35?

9. What will you do differently to *serve* your wife and children more specifically?

10. Ephesians 6:4 says fathers need to be *nurturing*. Tell in what ways you plan to be more nurturing with your children.

Study Eight
Spiritual Warfare

You awaken in the night and hear breaking glass. Half asleep, you fumble for your glasses. Then silence. Were you dreaming? Should you get up?

Suddenly, a shadow slips past your bedroom door, stealthily creeping down the hall toward your children's room. You bolt out of bed, forgetting all fear, thinking of nothing but how to defend your family from this intruder.

Searching frantically for a weapon, you remember your son's baseball bat standing in the corner. You grab it, then notice your wife still peacefully sleeping.

"Honey, wake up!" you hiss, shaking your wife. "Someone's in the house. Call 9-1-1. I'm going after him before he hurts the children!"

Only seconds after the shadow slides past your room, you're in the hall, gripping the bat tightly. You flip the light switch, taking away the intruder's safe haven of darkness.

"God, protect my children," you whisper, throwing open one door after another. You reach for the knob of your office door. Suddenly, a sickening crash to your left startles you.

You throw open the door and cold air hits your face. The computer is lying smashed on the floor. Papers are strewn everywhere. And the intruder has escaped through the broken window.

Dressed in nothing but pajamas — angry now instead of afraid — you jump through the open window just in time to see the intruder rush into the alley. You chase him, yelling for him to stop. He runs even faster.

He darts into a pitch-dark side alley and disappears. You can hear his footsteps as he continues to run away. After a moment's hesitation, you decide to return home. Your family is left unprotected. (Taken from *Heart of the Warrior*, pp. 73-74.)

I have no doubt that if the above ever happened to you, you'd come to the physical defense of your family in a heartbeat. But would you be so quick to come to their *spiritual* defense? Maybe you're even asking yourself, "What exactly is spiritual defensiveness?"

Good question. The answer is found in the Bible. Let's consider the following brief synopsis of Ephesians 6:10-12.

Understanding the Battle

* Our battle is *not* "against flesh and blood."

* Our battle *is* "against the rulers, against the authorities, against the powers of this dark world and against the spiritual forces of evil in the heavenly realm."

* These rulers and powers cause *demonic strongholds*.

Elsewhere in the Bible, Paul helps us distinguish between an earthly and a heavenly perspective of spiritual warfare in 2 Corinthians 10:3-5.

Earthly Versus Heavenly Defense

* ✱ "Though we walk in the flesh" — *earthly*
* ✱ "We do not war according to the flesh" — *heavenly*
* ✱ "Our weapons of warfare are not flesh" — *earthly*
* ✱ "But divinely powerful (mighty before God) for the destruction of strongholds" — *heavenly*

Spiritual defense is the acknowledgment of clashing kingdoms. When one becomes a Christian and actively seeks to reclaim his life or the spiritual territory surrounding his family he is invading the kingdom of Satan with the kingdom of God.

For years now, you may have been a non-Christian or religious instead of spiritual. Everyday, Satan has been actively seeking to gain new ground in your life in order that he might establish a stronghold there. His strategy is simple, but lethal: start with tempting a man to have an active fantasy life — wishing for something unattainable or forbidden. Move him from mere fantasy to active participation — that is, the actual acting out of the fantasy. Cause the acting out to become an obsession or habit and Satan has a STRONGHOLD on the man's life. He is no longer able to exercise free will, but is a slave to his passions and sinful appetites. He is, according to Paul, in bondage to demonic rulers, authorities, powers of this dark world, and spiritual forces of evil in the heavenly (or supernatural) realm.

The answer is *confession* and *repentance* and *accountability*. And then, we must "put on the full armor of God" (Eph. 6:10) that we might take our stand "against the devil's schemes"!

Picking Up the Armor

* Spiritual Weapon #1: PRAYER

* "And pray in the Spirit on all occasions with all kinds of prayers" (Eph. 6:18).

* Spiritual Weapon #2: THE WORD OF GOD

* "Take up the sword of the Spirit, which is the word of God" (Eph. 6:17).

It is our praying in the spirit that, according to J. Oswald Sanders, transacts its business in the sphere of the supernatural. Removed from the realm of the rational human mind, our prayers — assisted by the Holy Spirit (see Rom. 8:26) — occupy a strategic role "through which," says Sanders, "the victory gained on Calvary over Satan and his hosts reaches the captives and delivers them." Wow, now that's spiritual defensiveness!

Combine prayer with searching for God in his word, and you have an unbeatable combination. The perfect spiritual offensiveness — where you are on guard and ready to counterattack. We must remember, however, that Satan does not fear mortal man. In engaging the enemy in spiritual warfare, we need to do so *covered by* (see Ps. 140:7) and *in the name of* Jesus Christ as our protector and shield (see John 14:14; Ps. 3:3a). JESUS IS SATAN'S ONLY RIGHTFUL ENEMY. And it will be Christ in us, or in our midst when we gather in his name, that Satan is subject to — whether he likes it or not.

> Jesus did not wear armor, carry a sword or spend hours building his biceps. Instead, he spent all the years before and during his ministry building up a spiritual relationship with his Father.

> When the ultimate test against Satan came, he was

ready. He saved the world because of his submission to God — by his willingness to sacrifice everything for all believers.

Here is what it means, fathers, to heed the call to arms: you must give your lives willingly on behalf of your families. You must slay on God's altar that evil spirit of self that keeps you from putting God and your families first in your lives. You must die to yourselves, brothers, as Jesus did. And you must live for your wives and children.

"Be very careful, then, how you live — not as unwise but as wise, making the most of every opportunity, because the days are evil," Paul writes in Ephesians 5:15-16.

Fathers, God has given you the greatest opportunity in the world: to lead your families to Christ through your living example. He is calling us all, Christian brothers, to strengthen our own families so that we may bring Christ's light to the whole world. This book is for all of us who are trying hard to fight that "good fight" but seem to be losing ground. Its message is meant to provide you, as a father, with an arsenal of spiritual insights — a battle plan — that will enable you to fight that good fight in your home and turn the tide of demonic warfare being waged against all humanity.

Your armor is in place. Your sword is in hand. And as you raise your spiritual weapons against Satan, your heart is turned toward God in heaven and your family at home. With the strength of your faith and the support of your mighty prayer warriors, you are ready to crush the enemy.

The trumpet has sounded, men, and our crucified and resurrected general leads us into battle. We must heed the call to war today! (Taken from *Heart of the Warrior*, pp. 95-96.)

Reflecting on Study Eight

1. Consider the following synopsis of Immature Focus versus Mature Focus and relate it to what you have learned regarding the heart of a warrior.

Immature Focus Versus Mature Focus

Focus on *"getting saved"*	Focus on *being like Jesus*
Focus on *psychology*	Focus on *sanctification*
Rejects God's discipline	Receives God's reproach
Denies sin in the believer's life	Confesses sin before God

2. Read aloud Colossians 2:8. What is demonic bondage or captivity stated here?

3. Would you agree that the function of a demonic stronghold is to take away our free will — that is, imprison the heart and take hold of our minds and rule us?

4. A religious spirit (demonic stronghold) that has imprisoned the heart and controlled the mind is said to be predictable — for example, same buzz words or religious language, no new thoughts or ideas, and not open to rebuke. Do you agree or disagree? Explain.

5. What strongholds are in your life? Voluntarily explain.

6. It is said that a religious spirit in a man will empha-
   size the "new birth" — a one time event — and
   rarely focus on "new growth" which is ongoing.
   Would you agree and why?

7. Read Exodus 17 about Joshua, Aaron, Hur, and
   Moses and the army of Israel and relate it to the
   phrase, "It was what happened on the hilltop that
   determined what happened in the valley!" What are
   the possible implications for small groups of men or
   "warrior bands"?

8. Read John 16:11, 1 John 4:4, and 1 John 5:3 aloud.
   Why are these Scriptures a source of encouragement?

9. Hebrews 4:12 talks about our spiritual weapon #2:
   The Word. What do you think is the meaning of
   "living and active" and "sharper than any double-
   edged sword"?

10. How has this study helped open your heart and free
    your mind to the life of a spiritual warrior? Was it
    what you were expecting? In what ways was it dif-
    ferent? Would you recommend it to other brothers?
    Explain why.

ABOUT THE AUTHOR

Michael O'Donnell is widely recognized as an authority in the field of fathering and family studies. He serves as Chairman of the Board for International Family Life Institute, Inc. of Folsom, PA, Knoxville, TN, and Abilene, TX. Michael is also Adjunct Professor of Human Development and Family Studies at Abilene Christian University and is the Founder/Executive Director of the Southwest Center for Fathering in Abilene. He is the author of *Home From Oz*, published by Word Publishing in 1994. He is a graduate of Eastern Baptist Theological and Cincinnati Christian Seminaries and received his doctorate from Kansas State University. Dr. O'Donnell is a Charter Member of the American Association of Christian Counselors, President and Executive Board Member of the Texas Council on Family Relations, Member and State Coordinator for Family Life Certification, and a Member of the Council of Presidents for the National Council on Family Relations. He is married to Rachel and they have three children: Patrick, Kayla and Cara (deceased).